Life in Translation

Life in Translation

Azila Talit Reisenberger

ISBN: 978-0-9802729-1-8
© Azila Talit Reisenberger 2008

First published in 2008 by Modjaji Books
P O Box 385, Athlone, 7760
modjaji.books@gmail.com

Edited by Robert Berold
Printed and bound in South Africa by Creda Communications
Cover artwork: Hannah Morris
Book design by: Stuart-Clark & Associates cc
Author Photograph: Cliff Alexander

Earlier versions of some of the poems in this book were published in:
Carapes, Jewish Affairs, New Contrast, Shalom LA, CCAR (Central
Conference of American Rabbis), Psefas, and Mahut.

The Hebrew poems printed in this book were previously published in
2002 in Mahazor Ahava (Cycle of Love) by Gevanim, Tel-Aviv.

Acknowledgements

Many people helped me put my life into order in English. I thank them here:

Rachelle Mann who translated 'Yom Kippur' and 'Kaddish'. Riva Rubin who translated 'Shema' and 'Going Home'. And Immanuel Suttner who translated: 'Four daughters', 'Enough', 'Philomela', 'Creating', 'The thread of her life' and 'Violent death'. Immanuel also helped me to smooth the sharp 'foreign' corners in the poems, 'Table Bay Psalm' and 'Living in the Dictionary' which I wrote in 'Hebrewtised' English.

Then came Robert Berold who with love and wisdom culled the real meaning behind some of my peculiar expressions, and with ruthless honesty and intelligence helped me to put it in the best aesthetical way – in English.

A special thanks to Jared Keith Ginsburg, a young Cape Town artist for inspiring the cover design.

And lastly Colleen Higgs who believed that there is a diamond behind the rough stone she saw initially.

This book is dedicated
To You.

You enrich my life.

Contents

Everlasting Eve 11

You 12

Yom Kippur 13

Heritage 14

In the Beginning 16

Four Daughters 18

Sisterhood 19

Shema 20

Scent of Love 22

Going home 23

Heavy heart 24

Love 25

In the heat of the night 26

Silver anniversary 27

Class reunion 28

Not yet 29

Enough 30

Philomela 31

Creating 32

Your words 33

Writing poetry 34

The thread of her life 36

Some people's thoughts 38

Disappointment 39

Sacred thanks 40

Kaddish 41

Silent anguish 42

Violent death   43
Table Bay Psalm   44
Seven year itch   45
Wasted knowledge   46
Yiches   47
Teacher-woman   48
Naches   49
Whispering   50
Thanksgiving   51
Ten past the wedding   52
Five past menopause   53
Time of wisdom   54
Quarter to retirement   55
In Exile   56
In Between   58
You who live secure in your
    mother-tongue   59
Living in the dictionary   60

Notes to the poems   62
About the poet   64

Everlasting Eve

Years ago I saw my late mother
rising out of the bath tub;
her soft arms holding fast
assisting her veined legs
to rise out of the water.

She caught my gaze
resting on her sagging breasts
and her limp belly
and she said:
"That was your home, you know"
lowering her eyes in embarrassment.

Now it is I who climb out of the bath-water,
insulted by the stare of
the modern big mirror.

I dab my doughy stomach.
And already my daughter's smooth belly
stretches to house the next generation.

You

To my mother

The funeral with its sanctioned tears
is long gone.

I still walk to the phone,
and pick up the receiver
longing to hear your proud smile
when I share my little victories.

Instead, I go to the kitchen
to make dinner
and pretend it is the onion
that makes me cry

while you lie peacefully
in the earth.

Yom Kippur
Day of Atonement

For the sins committed against our parents –
      Ingratitude
      Indifference
      Wasting precious time
We shall have to wait
until our children
wipe clean the slate
with their sins.

Translated by Rachelle Mann

Heritage

The robe which I have inherited
from my parents
hangs
in the entrance hall.
Still,
I am too small to reach it.

יְרֻשָׁה

עַל וָו בַּפְּרוֹזְדּוֹר
תְּלוּיָה הַגְּלִימָה שֶׁהוֹרִישׁוּ לִי הוֹרַי,
וּקְטַנָּה אֲנִי עֲדַיִן —
עֲדֶיהָ.

In the Beginning

"And God said let us make human in our image, after our likeness...and God saw that it was good. And it was evening and it was morning the sixth day. Thus He finished... His work and... He rested". (GENESIS 1:26-2:2).

Alert and ready she lay
listening
to life created inside her
out of no graspable form and void.
A new world.
                    And she saw that it was good.

In her own image, after her own likeness
she created a new hope.
                    And she saw that it was good.

And it was evening and it was morning
And it is

הַתְחָלָה

שְׁכְבָה עֲרוּכָה, נְכוֹנָה,
הַקְשִׁיבָה
לַחַיִּים
הַמִּתְפַּתְּחִים בְּתוֹכָה
כְּמוֹ מִתֹּהוּ וָבֹהוּ,
עוֹלָם חָדָשׁ,
וַתֵּרֶא כִּי טוֹב.
בְּצַלְמָהּ וּבִדְמוּתָהּ
בָּרְאָה
תִּקְוָה חֲדָשָׁה
וַתֵּרֶא כִּי טוֹב.
וַיְהִי עֶרֶב וַיְהִי בֹּקֶר
וַיְהִי

Four Daughters

The Haggadah of Pessach teaches us that: "…The Torah alludes to four types of sons: one who is wise, and one who is wicked, one who is naive, and one who does not know how to ask" and together they comprise 'The People'.

Four daughters –
four walls of the home.

It's not that only one is wise
or one wicked,
one innocent,
and one unable to ask –

for not one of them is simple
and who better than they know to question?

They are four daughters
who are worthy of being spoken of

their stories
the stories
on the house their parents built.

And despite the differences
four walls may have,
they form the home.
Each one more complete
when they are together.

Sisterhood

When I sink low
in disappointment
heavily burdened with self doubt
my sisters hold me up.

They walk me up a staircase
that they created for me,
made of our loved childhood pictures,
of paper clippings of my success,
of my degrees
and above all,
pictures of all my loved and loving ones.

My sisters' faith in me
glues the stairs fast
and their shoulders
lift me up to the place
where even the last cloud
of self doubt dissipates.

Translated by Immanuel Suttner

Shema

The credo of Jewish faith: "Shema Israel... Hear O Israel...
you shall love the Lord your God with all your heart and with all
your soul and with all your might. And these words which
I command you this day shall be inscribed upon your heart...
recite them when you are at home and when you go out, when
you lie down and when you rise..." (DEUTERONOMY 6:4-7).

To Peter

You are with me
        when I lie down and when I rise,
You are with me
        when I go out and when I return,
You are One with me
        in every single cell.

My soul
- mate.

Translated by Riva Rubin

שְׁמַע

אַתָּה עִמִּי
בְּשָׁכְבִי וּבְקוּמִי,
אַתָּה עִמִּי
בְּלֶכְתִּי וּבְשׁוּבִי,
אַתָּה עִמִּי
"אֶחָד"
בְּכָל נְשִׁימָה
נְשַׁמְתִּי.

Scent of Love

Perfume of love
scents all around.
But it dissipates.

They tell us that it turns to
friendship
and partnership
and companionship.

We need not decry these;
but we cry for the perfume of love
when it goes.

Going home

The smile on my face
is a remembering smile
because I've already packed.
I'm on my way home.

The smile on my face
is an extension of the smile
in my head that flows from
the smile in my memory
of the kisses of your mouth,
the touch of your body
whose every line and facet
is stamped on my fingertips.

The smile on my face
was born of the memory of you
wrapping your arms around my neck,
saying, "I missed you."
Or even if not.
Even if you just call from the kitchen,
"Is that you?
"Great. I've been waiting."

I smile
and the smile
draws strands of happiness
in its wake.

I'm on my way home.

Translated by Riva Rubin

Heavy heart

Into our love abode I brought
a heavy heart,
laid it with my lame limbs
spooned into your big body.

Unto your warm lips
I passed
the sand of disappointment
gritting between my teeth.

And under your armpit,
I buried my head
emptied of my dreams.

You promised that by the end of the night
new dreams would rush in.
But I was too disappointed to believe you.

Love

In the hidden creases of my body
I carry my husband's potent love.
Smiling like a satisfied cat
I surrender my place
in the queue in Pick n Pay
to an angry woman.
And his smell on my fingers
that flick the pages
in the magazine
from the newspaper stand
brings a smile,
when I realize that
the romantic pictures in the magazines
are but a pale sham
of love.

In the heat of the night

When I watered
the dry parched soil
I listened to the gurgling
satiated sound
from the depth.
Like the bubbling sound of a
baby, sucking her toes,
Satisfied.
Pap. Pap. Pap.

Last night
I heard my body's gentle 'pap' 'pap'
as I walked bare feet
in the dark house.
You had fallen asleep and I
was on my way to the fridge
in search of water
to satisfy my thirst.

It was a hot night.

Silver anniversary

All the memories
of our years side by side
are hidden under the surface
of your beautiful eyes.

I dive into these
familiar trusted pools
when I need my life-pearls.

Class reunion

Once we were like
arrows in the same quiver
shot at shiny targets
set way ahead.

Now,
in a class reunion
thirty years on,
we sit around desks that are too small for us,
all thickened, blunted and aged
but each so individually different.
It is hard to believe
that we were so alike
as arrows in a quiver.

Then we were shot into the future.
Some arrows did not keep their route,
passing winds pushed them astray.
Some were flapping and flailing,
and flopped.
Some were non-starters,
or overshot their target.

Now we have all returned
for the class reunion,
each so individually different.

They sit us at the uniform desks,
trying to cram us
into the old quiver.

Not yet

The doctor's prognosis
was like my parents words:
"You go to sleep now".

Why must life go on without me?
Why must there be laughter and love -
when I am shunned into The Night?
Lying alone.
In the dark.

When there is no more life in me to fight or cry
I shall lie down like a child falling asleep over
her toys,
loosening my grasp over earthly possessions;
one by one
all my loved ones.

But I don't want to die yet
I still have it in me,
Le'Hayim.

Enough

Enough I said.
Enough rearing,
enough raising,
enough kissing,
enough soothing,
enough serving.

Enough I said.
Enough cooking,
enough washing,
enough bill paying,
enough home-making,
enough message taking,
and doctor's room waiting.

Enough I said.
I must conceive again.
Conceive myself.
Write.

Translated by Immanuel Suttner

Philomela

Long ago her life was filled with words.
and then she blossomed,
grew full of heart and soul.
A woman of beauty.
but above all else
beautiful poems rolled on her tongue.

And when her heart was snatched
she sang love
like a nightingale sings.
She sang and never knew

never knew she would be ruled
like Eve
and that, by the sweat of his brow,
he would build a home
and she would bear children
in pain.

never knew that the man
who pronounced them husband and wife
handed the man who delivered her babies
the scalpel upon which was engraved:
Philomela.

Translated by Immanuel Suttner

Creating

"My bowels, my bowels I writhe with pain, the chambers of my heart cry within me, I cannot hold my peace… o my soul…"
(JEREMIAH 4:19)

My bowels, my bowels, I writhe in pain
the chambers of my heart moan
like the depth of the earth.
Unsung
unheard
boiling.

My words erupt
from the furnace within,
my tongue is shod
by logic's sledgehammer,
behold, I am laid out, forged, before you.

Translated by Immanuel Suttner

Your words

Your words
were knives stuck into
the table in front of me
vibrating inside my
gut.

Writing poetry

Sometimes in the depth of the night
I am pulled out of my dreams
by Words –
words strung into lines of poems.
The Words sob at my ear
pleading with me to write them down.
If I try to push them away,
"I am tired,"
they tug tenaciously at my blanket
asking: if not you, who?
      If not now, when?

Sometimes when I just sit there
enjoying being
I am knocked off my peace
by angry Words –
words strung into lines of poems.
They kick my fragile quietitude
jab a finger at my brows
demand: Write us down.
      If not you, who?
      If not now, when?

Yet sometimes when
I am searching for Words
they elude me.
In frantic need
I look in dark corners;
under the bed;
even behind the curtains.
I can hear their sneering,
mocking my desperation
to string a line
while they would not reveal themselves.

But sometimes
in times of grace,
the Words
fall into my lap
strung eagerly into lines of poems.

And this is Wordly bliss.

The thread of her life

Once Arachne wove
her life's story:
her ripening nubile body,
adolescent joy
compassion for the underdog
ideas, idealism
a wondrous yarn.

Until Athena became jealous and sent her a
bridegroom.

And then she was trapped in the web of her life
the sorties to the park
the nappies, the swings
and children's stories;
snot and doctors,
ballet concerts
parent's evenings,
shopping and bills,
and chores
and chores and chores.
a spidery web
that wrapped itself
around her neck.

And they wove her a shroud.

Athena was repentant,
she hadn't known
how greatly Arachne loved to weave.

Her loved ones mourned
they hadn't known
that weaving was the thread
on which her life was hanging.

Translated by Immanuel Suttner

Some people's thoughts

Some people's thoughts
while they are silent
are like magnificent maple leaves
in autumn.
But when they fall
haughty people trample on them.

Some people's thoughts
while they are silent
are like foetuses
in a mother's womb.
And when they are born
they are celebrated and embraced.

All thoughts start
in silence.
They are
Silence's Splendour.

Disappointment

Disappointment
is like a slapping wind on the face.
The heart crumbling
grain by grain.
Sand between the teeth.
Even the mountain
loses its mighty features,
becoming blunt,
rounded
grounded,
grain by grain.

Disappointment.
Sand between the teeth.

Sacred thanks

My thanks to you my friend
are like the dough
that rises in your tenderness,
ready to be baked into the
warm, soft Sabbath bread
that sustains
body and soul.

Kaddish

(prayer for the dead)

Her sole sin was –
Lighting up.
A sin – not even the Great Healer
In the Yom Kippur Ward
Could pardon.
Now, inside the box
She stopped
Smoking.

Translated by Rachelle Mann

Silent anguish

From the top of the mountain,
the top of the world
the sun was so high with me
and the twinkle in the windows of far away houses
shimmered in the fresh warm air.

Then I was descending
into the valley of the shadow.
The sun sank low with me.
The shadows grew longer
and the valley grew darker,
fingers of mist wrapped me.

My mouth was wide open
like a fish frozen scream.
My throat could not send out voice,
nor cry for help.

Violent death

The birds of the soul
like black crows
their wings beating
beating and squawking
squawking and rising
hopelessly leaving
the clutching earth,
the ties of earthly love.

Dart and chatter
like crows
caught in the departure hall
that fly towards the light
and get caught by the window panes
without passports
flying nowhere.

Below, on the ground
wet-eyed
the mourners try
with their prayers
to tear an opening and
send the souls to salvation
and find some consolation for themselves.

Translated by Immanuel Suttner

Table Bay Psalm

Sailing in Table Bay
is like playing hide and seek with God,
and the seas of Good Hope,
echo the Psalm:

> "Behold the sea, great and wide;
> therein are moving things innumerable,
> living creatures both great and small."

The strings of my soul are plucked
anointed with the sense of privilege.
How blessed I am to witness,
and whisper the living words:

> "How manifold are thy works, O Lord,
> In wisdom You have made them all".

Seven year itch

"And God has finished on the seventh day His work which He had made, and He rested…" (GENESIS 2:2)

"Six years shall your slave serve you and in the seventh he shall go out free…" (EXODUS 21:2).

In the seventh year
he rested
from all his work and family,
washed his hands,
packed a suitcase,
and
left.

Wasted knowledge

The knowledge
gathered through years of
learning and life-experience
has highlighted rich grey
over my blonde;
and it is heart wrenching
that it is going to die with me.

Yiches

At rabbinical debates
when women's issues are ignored
and my wigless voice is silenced,
my father's yeshiva education
bolsters my voice,
makes their beards
sit up and take notice.

Teacher-woman

I walked into the classroom
with my vagina in my heart
and my PMS in my head.
I was following my breasts
sticking out like beacons
ahead of me.

'She is here'
went the loud whisper
and a pitter patter
fluttered around the class.

But the minute the class started
big curious eyes
were fixed to the blackboard
and eager ears
listened beyond my monthly voice.

The Teacher in me took over -
yet
the Woman
was sitting on my shoulder
smiling.

Naches

I take my children everywhere,
they are the glint in my eyes,
the wrinkles under it
and the crest of pride
on which I surf so high.

They are my source of information
about the clubs in Long Street,
the hidden trails on the mountain,
and the hip slang on my tongue
that makes my students smile.

Whispering

It is my six million brethren
       who hold my dentist's hand back
       lest he pulls my old gold tooth,
       Whispering in my ear
       "Remember our toothless mouths on the gallows"

       who hold my optometrist's hand back
       lest he discards my old pair of spectacles,
       Whispering in my ear
       "Remember the piles of glasses
       looking blindly at the gas-chamber".

       who hold my shoe saleslady's hand
       lest she throws my old pair away,
       Whispering in my ear
       "Remember the mountain of shoes
       testifying to our death-march
       that we walked soulless and barefoot".

       who hold my hairdresser's hand back
       when she lets my cut hair fall unto the floor,
       Whispering in my ear
       "Remember the mattresses made with our hair
       cut with our dreams straight out of our heads".

It is these six million Whispers
that direct my life.

Thanksgiving

Friday evening prayer: "Blessed art thou, O Lord, King of the universe who… with wisdom… arrangest the stars in their watches in the sky, according to thy will…"

Morning prayer for children, upon waking up: "Blessed art thou, O Lord our God living and eternal King who hast restored my soul unto me in mercy…"

I give thanks unto thee,
O living and eternal God,
who, in great wisdom
has arranged the stars
in their watches
to pour forth
illuminating sparks
and Hidden Light.

I give thanks unto thee,
O loving and eternal God,
who, in great mercy
hast bestowed upon me
a kaleidoscope for a soul
to observe and absorb the Light
and abounding seasons
to glow in it.

Ten past the wedding

The honeymoon is for-gone.
my love's smiling snores
are in perfect rhythm
with the heart-beat
and the soft kicking inside me.

Five past menopause

Half past awkward puberty,
and a quarter past frantic motherhood,
five past menopause.

The biological clock is ticking.

The body is a soft glove to the soul.
My womanhood clings to me
like a wet T-shirt.

Time of wisdom

Half past school,
quarter past degrees and diplomas,
and ten past life's lessons.

It is
five to forgetting
and
the clock is ticking faster.

Quarter to retirement

While we built a home
    degrees were taken
While I changed nappies
    mediocre colleagues passed me by,
While I loved our children's souls into shape
    books were written.
While I supported others,
    posts were filled.
And now,
at a quarter to retirement
    my time is running out.

In Exile

I fell off the bed.
The floor is hard and cold.

My heart longs
for the warm bodies
tucked together under the duvet.
Loving
like feathers
all so soft.

I am an outsider now.
Yearning to belong.

I fell off the bed.
Hard the floor and cold.
Hard and cold the diaspora.

בַּגּוֹלָה

נָפַלְתִּי מִן הַמִּטָּה.
קָשָׁה הָרִצְפָּה וְקָרָה.

עוֹרֵג לִבִּי
לַגּוּפוֹת הַחַמִּים
בֵּין הַמַּצָּעִים
אוֹהֲבִים
כִּפְלוּמַת נוֹצוֹת
רַכִּים, כֹּה רַכִּים.

רַק אֲנִי בַּחוּץ
כְּמֵהַּ לִשְׂמִיכָה.

נָפַלְתִּי מִן הַמִּטָּה.
קָשָׁה הָרִצְפָּה וְקָרָה.
קָשָׁה וְקָרָה כַּגָּלוּת.

In Between

Sitting on the veranda,
drenched by the jacaranda
that washes lilac the avenue
stretching ahead.
Friends passing by wave and
call out warm English greetings.

Echoes from within
steal from the window behind
lure my ears and coax my tongue
to join and hum
Hebrew lullabies from my distant cradle.

I am wedged in between,
as if trapped in a wheelchair
with stairs
both ahead and behind.

You who live secure in your mother-tongue

You who live secure in your mother-tongue,
consider this:

We vagabonds, who left our secure homes,
to roam the earth,
rest our heads in many dwelling places.
We are but visitors at your home.

We may know how to get to the kitchen,
we may know how to get to the bathroom,
but the small hidden nooks and crannies,
and the attics with memories of yore,
are out of our laborious reach.

Tired, tired we are.
Tired of playing translations,
forever bumping into articles
and language particles.

Yet, we sparkle your home
with gems from our childhood rhymes,
flashing fabricated words,
on your solid hardened walls.

You who have always stayed put and secure,
consider this:

You know not
when you have to leave your castles
and roam the earth.

Living in the dictionary

The philosophical question
'what is the meaning of my life'
does not send me to the books of the masters,
but rather to the dictionary.

The dictionary
gives me the meaning of 'meaning'.
In its pages my home in the Karoo
is placed right in the heart of the Negev
and my friendly boer neighbours
are called *chaverim*.

Forever I search the dictionary for my life,
try to work out
What am I to, for, and with
                            you:
Am I affiliated, attached or associated?
Am I linked, annexed or merged?
Surely not amalgamated.
Is there a word for the wish to belong?

I am validated only through
being mediated
in the dictionary.
And the nuances
in the recess of my heart,
are edited by a diligent editor
who ensures that I am described as:
connected with,
working for,
relevant to
and always so eagerly
waiting to be accepted by –
                         you.

Notes to the poems

Not yet – (p29) *Le'Hayim* means literally: "To Life." it is a spontaneous exuberant call when one toasts somebody or at a time of celebration.

Philomela – (p31) in *Metamorphoses* Ovid tells the story of Philomela (Princess of Athens) who was raped. In order to shut her up, the rapists cut off her tongue. Other versions of the story tell how Philomela turned to a nightingale and thus continued to sing her life story, in spite of losing her tongue.

Today Philomela is a symbol to all women who endure the suffering inflicted on them by the patriarchal system, yet find a way to triumph and tell their stories against all odds.

Table Bay Psalm – (p44) the quotes are taken from the Book of Psalms, chapter 104, verses 25 and 24.

Yiches – (p47) means 'geneological records'. In Jewish religious circles one's Yiches, which can be seen as "pedigree", is very important, as it determines whether you are Jewish in the eye of the Halacha, i.e. the Jewish law. The more observant or knowledgeable person is, the better is his or her Yiches.

Naches – (p49) is a Yiddish term that describes the immense pleasure and pride that a Jewish mother obtains from her children.

Thanksgiving – (p51) On waking up in the morning every Jew thanks God for being alive. Children express it in a naïve way, thanking God for bringing back their soul after He took it to heaven to be with Him during the night. Men on the other hand have a less naïve prayer, they don their prayer shawl and they thank Him for the abundant graces He bestowed upon them, one of which is Not making them a woman (!) This is a hurtful issue for Jewish women, some of whom have developed an aversion to the morning prayer. In this poem the poet subverts her inferior position as a woman and goes on to magnify God's name and thank Him – as she feels she is special.

Hidden Light, as is known by its *Kabbalistic* term: *Ha'Or Ha'Ganuz* is God's shards of light which are found in the world and have to be redeemed by Human Grace. The *Zohar*, which is the book on which the Kabbalah is built, tells us that when God finished the creation of the world He sent forth His spirit to fill in the world, but His spirit was so immense that it shattered the physical world into tiny little shards. When the world was created again, God limited His spirit before He sent forth His spirit to fill the world, and this time all was well. But the shards of God's spirit from the original created world are lying here on earth in the form of Hidden Light. When any person on earth performs any act of goodness one of these sparkles of the Hidden Light are redeemed and the original world with the greatness of God's full magnificent spirit is redeemed, and the world is a holier place.

Living in the dictionary – (p60) *chaverim* is the Hebrew word for friends.

About the poet

Azila Talit Reisenberger is an award winning author who has had poetry and short stories published in Israel, the USA, UK, Germany and South Africa. Two of her plays: "Adam's Apple" and "The loving father", were staged at the Grahamstown Festival.

She is a senior lecturer in Hebrew and Jewish Studies in the School of Languages and Literatures at the University of Cape Town, and renowned for her passionate lectures and articles on gender issues and feminist theology in the Bible.

For the past 17 years she has served as the Spiritual Leader of Temple Hillel, a progressiveJewish community in East London. She lives in Cape Town with her husband and three children.